Psalm

Dedication

For Gladys

Psalm

Peter Owen Jones

BOOKS

Winchester, UK
Washington, USA

Copyright © 2005 O Books
46A West Street, Alresford, Hants SO24 9AU, U.K.
Tel: +44 (0) 1962 736880 Fax: +44 (0) 1962 736881
E-mail: office@johnhunt-publishing.com
www.johnhunt-publishing.com
www.0-books.net

U.S.A. and Canada
Books available from:
NBN,
15200 NBN Way
Blue Ridge Summit, PA 17214, U.S.A.
Email: custserv@nbnbooks.com
Tel: 1 800 462 6420
Fax: 1 800 338 4550

Text: © 2005 Peter Owen Jones

Design: Text set in Sabon by Nautilus Design

ISBN 1 903816 91 2

Printed by Tien Wah Press

Contents

————●●————

————●●————

Preface

The Psalms are about relationships. The relationship between God and you, between human beings and the environment, between wonder and fear, light and dark, connectedness and disconnectedness, good and evil, between words and silence.

Those of us who attempt to wedge the divine experience into words always fall short. We can never really do it, at best we can only show you the light from the diamond not the diamond itself. The way in which this light is described is going to change, thank God, with each generation as vocabulary and meaning mutate with the process of discovery and understanding. As human beings we inhabit an active state of creation, the image of God never dries. This means that no one generation can claim to speak for God at the expense of another.

I wanted to see what the Psalms would feel like in the language we in our generation are familiar with. I used many different translations to try and see them from as many different angles as possible. In attempting to recast just eleven of the Psalms and the 'Song of Simeon', they have become for me the language used by our forefathers, which takes the experience of God right to the edge of the expressible. The Psalms recount what divine experience feels like, written from the realm of prayer. At their heart is a complete trust in the existence of God and therefore the original authors feel they are able to be completely themselves. What actually sings through is raw, hurting, awe-struck humanity and an understanding of what the presence of God feels like as a human being. How God makes you feel. You enter this world of feelings in the Psalms. Once you go inside them, in through the words I found that David and Solomon are not so very far from us. They use different tools, different metaphors but their feelings, their questions; their struggle are the same as ours. I hope I have trodden lightly over this land, which is not mine; thankfully it has become common ground.

Thank you to the countless songwriters who have and continue to inspire. There are I think, some contemporary Psalms, 'Beautiful Day' by U2, Coolio's 'Gangsters'Paradise' but they are few and far between.

I would like to find more. Thank you to John Burnside for every word. The Cambridge Poets who encouraged me to keep going, Marina Yedigaroff for her letters, Adnams brewery for its ale, to Harlton church on Monday mornings, Alan Burles for the cover, Dr Nicholas Branson, Dr Mike Sayers and Rodney Barton for their wisdom, Nick Hammond for Riviera Siesta, Gladys Gott for her love and light and to Jenny Tombs who typed this all into shape. And to you who illuminated the experience of love, measured in distant engines, collecting hammers and robins.

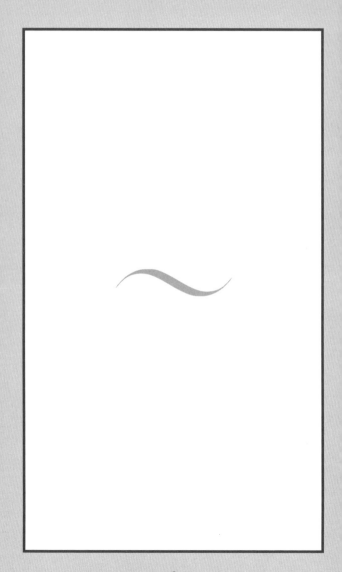

Psalm 121

———◦•◦———

I am here once more with the horizon
asking for answers, help even.

You find me again and I see
stars and days waiting for me to arrive.

You, the unceasing shepherd of the sleeping,
never seem surprised to see me,
you have always been awake to the world.

I wipe the sky from my eyes

and see your shadow beside me in the sun,
the hand that brings me back from the moon,

taking the bullets coming through the glass of
my room,

Forever beginning,
forever ending.
Forever becoming.

Psalm 19

The universe is one voice,
one spark that lights the countless skies.

One tide of nights and days
sing one praise,

speak one tongue.
The fluent stars respond.
Emptiness understands and

the rodeo electron
the release of inspiration
the mouse breathing
the rising flame
is one motion.

You, Lord, reared the naked sun
in this grove in space.
Swelling on desire
and a passion to prevail.

The light feeding the turning earth,
generating energy into the greed of new life,
erupting from the dust and rocks.

And all I know of you revives my soul
as I am drawn into truth and the soil of wisdom.

Your spiritual direction is a lesson in laughter.
You say "look inside for the light in your eyes
and

in all things I will endure, in your hope, in
your fear."
Your truth springs clear to the depth of your
words

which say more than all I can desire.
They are sweetness in my mouth

as I learn to free my anxious self
and accept the weightlessness of beauty.

Show me the ruins of the soul,
the easy roads of un-being,
everything that I have stained,

the smoke of self-delusion where I hide
my rewards and excuses.
All I've gained through lies is stolen
and I will give back the bribes I've taken.

May all the words of my mouth be prayer,
the meditations of my heart
where I learn your delight.

Psalm 142

———— •• ————

Now I cry to you, Lord, with all I have left
I finally speak your name out loud,

lay my pain once more down at your door.

As I fall, drawn into this spiral to the center
of another dark cloud, you know this place
without light, I've been here before, convinced
it's all I deserve.

There is nobody who can hear this inner pain on these streets full of strangers, I am one of them.

Exhausted by fear,
can't you hear me beside you stammering the whereabouts of wolves, who gather round this dying fire. They see a liar, they know I am not that strong.

Lead me out from this night, let me live so that I might thank you, say you rescued me, and those who speak your name agree in quiet prayer.

Psalm 65

———— •••• ————

Our hearts beat your name in this land,
our lips promise you in this city.

You absorb all that is prayer.
You are intimate with every strand of life

wasted with doubt, cracked with sin,
you feel from within these winters of guilt.

Those on the tracks of their inner self
hear you saying that everything is blessed,
and yes they fill worlds with your words.

And all the questions we ever ask
spin in the compass of all you know,
you answer in waves from the ends of the earth,
this relentless store.

You made the mountains,
laid down each rock with your hands.

You calm the storms, the breakers drown
and cities stand quiet before you.

Listening to those torn to the edges,
talking to angels no one else believes,
ranting the wonderful prophesies in each
dusk and dawn.

"You fill the rivers.
You ripen the grain on the stem,
this banquet you bring.

You pour out the rain, feeding the soil,
simmering down all the sharp plough leaves,
loading the fields
with seed upon seed.

Each year your plenty is reborn
as you throw your crown into
ditches and thorns.

The land sings out beyond the fences
and the hills decked in horizons call

and the meadows bringing on
ewes and lambs and the velvet valleys
the crowds of corn
stand and shout for joy I am."

Psalm 90

—•●•—

From beginning to beginning you have been
our sanctuary,

before you spun the mountains,
heeled the soil into the land,
cried from earth to earth I am.

You lay me down in the grave,
untangle me from an age of memories.

Your yesterday is a thousand years,
a candle in the early hours.

We slip through your dream in a hurry to live.

Like tender shoots from the morning's rain,
giving sap to the grain, then dying of thirst.

We choose comfort before justice
and cannot shake the hearse before us.

You know how we intend to scar,
to penetrate with fear.
You lay bare the grinning gangsters' plans.

Every hour your anger weighs us down
until we sigh with relief in death.

Oh we'll live seventy, eighty strong years,
maybe more; too long when you're working
and crying them away, too short to notice
what they were.

Just another day in the Hikhikomori Hotel
trying to break your silence with a broken bell.

Teach us to accept our impermanence,
to learn this is wisdom.

Come back to us, Lord;
you feel so far away, we
wait all day for your voice.

When will you wake us with singing,
calling delight into the days to come?

Leave us a residue of joy from
the hard times you heaped upon us;

these years dissolved in pills.

Refuel our senses with all you reveal
there in the wonder of our children's eyes.

So that these streets and fields bless us in your
name,
and all that we make is your praise with our
hands.

Psalm 23

You have found me yearning
now there is nothing else I need.

In your hands lies my seed of grass
earthed in your still image.

My soul breathes again, here on this highway
I will write your name.

And every piece of pain I have enclosed
you have known, and at last
I am not ashamed, and so

you lay down to quench the tide that spits
against me,
you make me beautiful, the bride of your
wine.

Yes, I will drink from this rich yield of love
each new day.
I will stay by your side,
your lamb in these fields.

Psalm 4

You can hear my inner voice.
I know you fathered goodness
and released me from another darkness.
And then I began to understand
how limitless I grew,
how I already knew this prayer.

And the rest of you,
your heads bowed before magazines,
paying your own tribute to human being,
so you shoot to nail me with those lies you
believed.

But I have felt divine love.
I have been heard.
I have spoken without needing words.

How many mothers you dreamt dead with
your triggers
is how many brothers you lost.
You're counting the cost in sleeping pills,
you are ill with anger.
Be still and know you are not a stranger to the
Lord.

There will always be those voices saying "if
only
we were rich" and "what does this distant god
care,
his face turned away from here."

But you, Lord, have poured your happiness in,
so much richer than the times I forgot to
worry,
safe in some flimsy plenty,
and soon I will sleep, lie down in your peace,
which is freedom without fear.

The Jubilate

Allah akbar praise the Lord
so many notes one accord
this prayer revolving the song
never sleeping here on earth

in heaven. This is the calling,
the yearning, raising the dust of being
into feeling and knowing, redeeming
every door and field.

And yes now is the time when your house
will yield such music, when every tongue
unbound
is alive with thanks,

for all that goodness endures.
For every hand held out.
For these sweet tears
and what is found in every truth.

Psalm 139

———•••———

Lord you know me completely,
you know when I sit, when I stand,
each grain of thought in the land
of my inner world.

All the journeys I've steered,
the road breaks in those half-
remembered bars,
you were there in every mile.

Every word I have spoken
is kept in your silence.

Your hand throws off the crows,
calms the cancerous cells.

I still choose to disregard each wonder,
clinging to the bars of my cage, afraid
of the ever-present end.

But you are before me,
within me,
beneath me,
beyond me.
There is nowhere apart from your presence.

If I find heaven you are there. You are there
in the swarm of my fear and hell.

Your hand held out when I wake on the sand
of my farthest shores,

waiting for me in the depths of my darkest
hours,

filling the night with your day.
You say the man and the womb are one,
there is no darkness between them.

You divided my first cell,
wrapped me in my mother's uterine wall.

Now I am the resonance of your prayer,
knowing creation.

I was your unborn child
with fins and unfinished hands
in a land I did not know.

You knew each line on the soles of my feet
as I lay like a book within my mother's womb.
My sapling arms sprung from an empty room.

Now you search for me with all your
thoughts.
They are innumerable.

Can I count each nucleus of dust
spilling from every star in all the strands of
time,
are they mine to know forever?

And you can burn those who haunt this town
with their looks and their fists,
those who taunt me when I pass
leave me alone.

Out on the corners they trade in spite,
talk a big fight, run a knife through your
name.

I hate those who hate you,
as they record their excuses
for all they are taking.

I hate them
with every train of thought,
with all my pain.

Look inside me, all these feelings
rising, falling on the tides of my mind.

Show me all that I hide,
the flesh fears time,
another two o nine in the everlasting days.

Psalm 12

Help me Lord, I stand alone.
All who believe in you are
dissolved in fiction and stones.

Everyone else is in disguise,
touting and yelling their reputation
with lies and spin.

Break their teeth.
Lay your wreath in every hollow claim.
They sound the same.

"Feel this tongue,
watch my lips
licking the wordsmith's fingertips."

But you Lord say "I hear the poor crying,
the oppressed dying by degrees each day
and I will rise and stand at their side."

These pure words
rise through the heat of time.

Watch our backs
on the streets of this town where

innocence is the easiest kill and the
truth is being sold for glitter and swill.

The Nunc Dimittis

Lord, the waiting is over
I can lie down in peace
and let this body go,
knowing your word is truth and

I have seen you human,
the unfurling of meaning,
your pregnancy in all that has being.

Illuminating every conscious self
with every moment of your birth.

Psalm 43

— ●●● —

Speak to me Lord,
through their words that cut like shards.
Hold me as I slip
on the smooth surface of deceit.

You are my peace and you are gone.
I walk through this town alone,
carrying the weight of the soil on my grave.

Where is your light, your truths
breaking into my shadows,
the summit of the solitude we shared,

the giver who led me into joy and delight,
the music I found in your name?

I have become a stranger to myself,
nervous of everything in focus.

Whatever happens, put your trust in the Lord.
I will find the rhythm of praise again,
walk through the door to the child once more.